Economic Evangelist

Economic Evangelist

◆

Helping people to become financially literate!

Gary Mayes

iUniverse, Inc.
New York Lincoln Shanghai

Economic Evangelist
Helping people to become financially literate!

iUniverse, Inc.

For information address:
iUniverse, Inc.
2021 Pine Lake Road, Suite 100
Lincoln, NE 68512
www.iuniverse.com

Economic Evangelist helping people to become financially literate.

Scripture quotations are taken from New King James Version of the Bible.

For emphasis, the author has placed Bible quotations in Bold print.

ISBN: 0-595-31605-0

Printed in the United States of America

Jerry & Clara Mayes

To my parents thank you for taking
me to Church at a young age and
believing in me.

Contents

Acknowledgments

First and foremost I would like to thank my Lord, my Savior, and my source Jesus Christ. Without Christ, I realize that I am nothing. I would also like to thank my anointed wife, Elizabeth for being by my side and putting up with me. Beside Jesus you are the best thing that has came into my life. To my father and mother, Jerry and Clara; I love you both and thank you for leading me in the right direction. To my brothers and sister Mike, Curtis and Tilara. I love you and very proud to call you my brother and sister. To my Pastor Glenn Rogers I love you and thank you for not only being my pastor, but an awesome friend as well. To my cousin and good friend Correy Teague thank you for being someone I can always talk to and share the word of God with. Finally to everyone else who has attended my workshops and gave me words of encouragement, I love you and thank you so much for being instruments of God.

Introduction

❖

Economic Evangelist

It's the 21st century and people are still slaves. Slaves in their mind and slaves to what America calls a **"job"**. It's what I call **"Just over broke"**. Fortune 500 companies are closing, laying-off, CEO's robbing and deceiving shareholders. It does not matter if you work for IBM, Microsoft, or McDonalds you get the picture, (seems) everybody economically are suffering the highest level of employment trouble. But I am writing this book to give you some good news. There is a paradigm—shift of wealth coming your way. The shift is moving from the wicked into the "Righteous" hands of faithful believers in Jesus Christ. God is calling you to be Kings & Queens in the marketplace. What is the marketplace? Well I am glad you ask. The marketplace is where people spend 98% of their time and have their being, at their workplace or home. The wealth of the wicked is laid up for you, yes you King & Queen. Not to be wealthy and sit on the seat of do nothing, but to be an example for Christ by going into the hedges and highways to minister salvation as well as, **financial salvation**. But only if you are in position financially. This book will change your mind on how money works, and tech you to "Stop working for money, and letting money work for you". The reason why there is such high unemployment is so God can shift you, his Kings & Queens into your rightful position. Where is that? The head and not the tail, as business owners and CEO's. Only those who are seeking **kingdom business** will reap the benefits.

The foundation of this movement is found in **Matthew 6:33, "Seek first the kingdom of heaven and all his righteousness, and all these other things will be added unto you"**. God has given us power to get wealth, so we might establish **His covenant** here on **earth**. The wealth He is talking about is not just money, but His word. For those of you who still have not caught what God is doing, let me break it down to you in lay-mans terms? Have you ever been in an organization or business? When the chaos begins to intensify, people begin to get missing all around you. Well look around it's happening now on your job or Church. Well the bible says, **"He that have an ear let him hear what the spirit is saying to the Church"**. The point I am trying to make is, if you're in tune with God, and you have been faithful, God is moving you into your wealthy place as an example for the world as well as the Body of Christ. God is trying to give you better when it seems like the bottom has falling out. Why? Because God has given you favor.

I am writing this book not to gain wealth, but God has burden me with a **specific need**. Even though it's talking about money it's not all about money, but to give God all the glory. Secondly to open up the mind of the believer on how Gods money works. Third, to challenge the believer to come forth, as the head and not the tail, to become the lender and not the borrower. Last but not least, to awaken that **"Lazarus"** business idea God has put inside of you. It's your covenant right to be financially blessed so you can do more ministry.

1

The shift from industrial age to the information age.

So why are so many people in the Body of Christ and sinners struggling financially? The bible says, in Hosea 4:6, "**My people are destroyed for the lack of Knowledge**". This sentence is were most people stop reading. But let me tell you it's not because of the lack of knowledge, it's the next sentence which says, "**Because you have rejected knowledge, I also will reject you from being <u>priest</u> for Me; Because you have forgotten the law of your God, I also will forget your children.** Think about it, which taught you about money, and how it works, your parents, high school or college? The school system or this world's system teaches you how to become a good employee, not an employer. Did you know that the world that impoverished you will not empower you? Have you ever heard that what you don't know won't hurt you. Well let me tell you what you don't know will hurt you. God does not change, but God is a God of change. My point is people of today (21st century) are still stuck in old *TRADI-TION. Meaning* still having church, making a living as they did back in the 60's, 70's and 80's. For example, people call themselves evangelist, but never leave outside of their churches four walls. It's no longer about the church; it's about the Kingdom. Meaning its time to stop just going to church, but being the church. Getting outside of your comfort zone, and out into the hedges and by-ways and highways, as a life-style, not just on Wednesday evening if that and Sunday morning. We think we are having real church. In the book of Acts they went from house to house breaking bread. Where do you have church most of the time? You do know that we are the church, not the church building? Are you a Christian or Christ like? God gave us a charge, **"Go ye therefore and teach all nations"**. For example: If you where in sales, and you sold houses. You attend all the top sales **information** meetings and seminars on selling houses every week. But you never go out to show any houses or talk about them. Do you think you would make any sales? Don't be secret agents? You must tell people the goodness of **Jesus**; you must tell people you sell houses, I hope your getting the picture. Same with making money, people are still making money the hard way not the smart way. Working for money instead of money working for them. As you read on this will make more since to you. This book will help you change your method, but not the message. Well what's the message? The message is that only working Gods program, and changing with Gods trends, will give you financial freedom. I found out that fear (FALSE, EVIDENCE, APPEARING, REAL), keeps a lot of people in the old way of doing things. Let me tell you fear is not of God, but Faith is. Faith is the substance of things hope for, and the evidence of things not seen. Your faith in Jesus Christ is your keys to financial success.

As I stated earlier, God and Gods word does not change, but God is a God of change. My point in saying this again is. Today I find so many people struggling, often working harder simply because they cling to old ideas. They want things to be the way they were; they resist change. I know people who are losing their jobs or their houses, and they blame technology or the economy or their boss. I am sad they failed to realize that they might be the problem. My good friend and brother in Christ, Pastor Glenn Rogers has a book entitled, "Could the number one enemy be me?" A powerful book dealing with you. But I am here to tell you the world does turn. The shift has already been made; did you shift with it? The shift I am talking about is from the **Industrial age** to the **Information age** in which we live today. Land was wealth 300 years ago. So the person who owned the land owned the wealth. Then, it was factories and production, and America rose to dominance. The industrialist owned the wealth. The same goes with your spiritual life. In Matthew 13:44, It talks about the parable of the hidden treasure saying, **"Again, the kingdom of heaven is like treasure hidden in a field, which a man found and hid; and for joy over it he goes and sells all that he has and buys that field"**.

The Holy Spirit reveled to me in this parable, that the field represents your flesh, and the treasure is the gift that God has invested inside of you. Meaning until you get your flesh under subjection, then will He release the treasure that is hidden inside of you. "**Greater is He that is <u>in me</u> than he that is in the world**". Don't you know that God does not dwell in an unclean place?

Today, wealth has shifted into **information**. The person who has the most timely information owns the wealth. The problem is information flies all around the world at the speed of light (Internet). Boundaries and borders as land cannot contain the new wealth and factories were. I have bible to back it up.

Ephesians 3:20 says, "Now to Him who is able to do exceedingly abundantly above all that we ask or think, according to the power that works in us." There will be a dramatic increase in the number of new godly multimillionaires. There also will be those who are left behind, because they would not change. What have you decided, bondage or blessings, Heaven or Hell?

God was a smart worker, how do I know? Well when you first open up the bible, God was working, but smart. In the beginning God created the heavens and the earth. How did he create them? He created them with his mouth by speaking. God had many titles, zoologist, chemist, and biologist but just to name a few. Then He turned around and created male and female, me and you to be co-labors with Him to carry out His work. Have you ever recognized God as the ultimate leader? Not only did He create the universe, redeem humankind, innovate with **entrepreneurial** energy, and act as a maverick He also leads. God could have ruled and redeemed planet earth on his own, but He chose to include us (**other people)** in his plans to lead.

2

Evangelist Leaders

Leaders aren't supposed to do all the work of a business or church. But are to effectively broker the talent on their team. Good teams use every gift and enjoy both unity and diversity. 1 Corinthians 12:4-7 says, "**There are diversities of gifts, but the same spirit. There are differences of ministries, but the same Lord. And there are diversities of activities, but it is the same God who works all in all. But the manifestation of the spirit is given to each one for the profit of all**". Leaders must build a team spirit that celebrates diversity. Teams must share a common goal, but not the same gifts. Teams mature when the leader insists on diversity and celebrates what everyone does together. Mike Murdock says "You should be were you are celebrated, not were you are tolerated". Healthy leaders often partner with others to reach their goals. In fact, we live in an age of partnership, both in the corporate world and in the church. Good partnerships do not foster **codependence independence**, but **interdependence**. Every party feels secure, is stretched, and enjoys synergy. The partnership multiplies the productivity of both parties. What I am trying to say is, "**Do not be unequally yoked together with unbelievers. For what fellowship has righteousness with lawlessness? And what communion has light with darkness?**" As an economic evangelist, your job is to lead as an example first, before you try to lead anybody or team. How can you teach someone about becoming debt free if your debt is not in order? The same goes for your spiritual life. Not saying you don't have bills or problems, but your debt to income and issues must come into order. Debt to income determines your wealth. If you make $50,000 a year and your debt is only $15,000, you are wealthy. But as I stated in the introduction wealth is not just money, but having a balance in your life, mind body and soul. The problem with the Body of Christ is we think that to be wealthy, you have to be a millionaire. But I am here to bust your bubble everybody is not going to be a millionaire. But to live like one you must become **<u>financially literate</u>**.

3

Financial Intelligence

Financial intelligence is simply having more options. If the opportunities aren't coming your way, what else can you do to improve your financial position? If a business opportunity lands in your lap and you have no money, and you have bad credit and can't get a loan. What else can you do to get the opportunity to work in your favor? How can you take nothing and turn it into a **cash flow system**. This is financial intelligence, by the help of the Holy spirit. It is not so much what happens, but how many different financial solutions you can think of to turn nothing into something. It is how you are solving financial problems, which is the problem most people have. Most people only know one solution: **work hard**, **save** and **borrow**. If you are the kind of person who is waiting for the "right" thing to happen, you might wait for a long time. The bible says," **Faith without works is dead**". The single most powerful asset we all have is our mind. If it is trained well, it can create enormous wealth in what seems to be an instant. Bishop Kevin L. Long has a powerful book called "The Gideon Principle" how one man changed his mind, after reading this book your mind should never be the same. But an untrained mind can also create extreme poverty that lasts lifetimes by teaching it to your families. "**A good man leaves an inheritance to his children's children, but the wealth of the sinner is stored up for the righteous**". Are you a victim, or are you the poison? This is why I invest in my financial intelligence, developing the most powerful asset I have. As an economic evangelist you want to be moving forward, not left behind. I can't say it enough, continually develop your financial intelligence because at each market change, some people will be on their knees begging for their jobs like today society. Others, meanwhile, will take nothing that life hands them, and turn nothing into thousands and maybe millions. That's **financial intelligence**.

www.maycomm.cjb.net

4

Use your job to build ASSETS!

Today I am not only a business investor, but I work for the American City Business Journal. Making on top of my business $30,000 a year. Why? As you read on in the book I will show how you get tax advantages for owning a business to offset all those deductions from your check! As a matter of fact after you read this book and start your home-based business I will show you how to get an INSTANT pay increase on your job without asking your boss!

But the main reason I am working at ACBJ is not what you're thinking, "job security" or benefits. But to **learn and earn**, also to get the inside game of corporate America for my own business. The next big reason is to take my check from my job as leverage to build up my **assets**, investing back into the Kingdom and my business that is virtually on autopilot. Developing assets helps me from being "just over broke", and diligently mass as much money as possible to build up my portfolio. Each dollar in my asset column represents an **employee** working hard to make more money. If you use your job as an asset then you will have options, to just build up your assets and quit the rat race way before "65" or "70". But my whole hearts desire is to minister **salvation** as well as **financial salvation**. So far it is working, many people on my job come to me just to talk. At the same time, asking questions about changing there finances or to say just pray for me. Also at the end of this book there are testimonies, one in particular is a young man who works with me. He one day overheard me talking about business and came over to me and ask what all I do. I shared with him about the healthcare benefits, then I started talking about how you can challenge things on your credit and get them deleted. To make a long story short he did not believe or know this could be done until I gave him the **"Information"** and he applied it and within 30 days he had repossession removed from his credit report. Now that's economic evangelism. But not only was I talking the game, I showed him "fruit" from my credit report were I had a loan removed. I am all the time dropping financial nuggets with a word right behind it. The bible says, **"Go ye therefore and teach all nations"**. Are you willing to spread the good news in the marketplace? The **greatest asset** I expect to happen while I am there, is to see **souls saved**.

5

Marketplace Instructions

✦

Proverbs 10:22

As a marketplace evangelist, God gives us some practical instructions on the use of money. An economic evangelist not only needs to know how to lead people to Christ. But be able to lead people to financial salvation. Some people are what the bible says, **"So heavenly bound, that there no earthly good"**. People in the marketplace and your Church lacks **financial literacy**. God will supply you with the personal and financial abilities to respond to the needs of others. If we all realized how God has blessed us and used our resources to do Gods will, hunger and poverty would be wiped out. Wealth is a blessing only if we use it in the way God intended. The bible says, **"The blessing of the Lord brings wealth, and He adds no trouble to it"**. The word of God also says, *"He who gathers little by little gathers much"*. As economic evangelist we must heed to the advice from God.

*Be generous in giving (11:24-25)
"One man gives freely, yet gains even more; another withholds unduly, but comes to poverty. "A generous man will prosper; he who refreshes others will himself be refreshed".

*Place people's needs ahead of profit (11:26)
"People curse the man who hoards grain, but blessing crowns him who is willing to sell".

*Be cautious of countersigning for another (17:18)
"A man lacking in judgement strikes hands in pledge and puts up security for his neighbor".

*Don't accept bribes (17:23)
"A wicked man accepts a bribe in secret to pervert the course of justice".

*Help the poor (19:17)
"He who is kind to the poor lends to the Lord, and He will reward him for what He has done".

*Store up for the future (21:20)
"In the house of the wise are stores of choice food and oil, but a foolish man devours all he has ".

*Be careful about borrowing (22:7)
"The rich rule over the poor, and the borrower is servant to the lender".

6

Kings and Queens in the Kingdom

What is the kingdom? Kingdom means to rule or to realm and has dominion over. God's kingdom is a place of peace, joy and understanding also godly authority to bring down satins kingdom. The kingdom of God is for everybody, but only the ones who receive and believe in God (Jesus). It's our job as believers to reach out to the lost, plant the seed and let God do the watering. Matthew 13: 23 says, **"But the one who received the seed that fell on good soil is the man who hears the word and understands it. He produces a crop, yielding a hundred, sixty or thirty times what was sown".** The kingdom of heaven is not a geographic location, but a spiritual realm where God rules, and where we share in His eternal life. We join that kingdom when we trust in Christ as our savior. Also the bible talks about the kingdom of God being like a mustard seed. The mustard seed to me represents Economic Evangelist. As economic evangelist you are going to start out with a small beginning, but as you begin to spread Gods word it will grow and produce great results. Who is an economic evangelist? Kings and Queens striving for perfection. No one is perfect. Let me give you an example. Just about everybody has a cellular phone. Cellular phones are messed up. Does not matter what company your with all cellular phones drop calls, and it is a billion dollar per year industry. What does that tell you? It tells you that you don't have to be perfect, and you can make a lot of money and you don't have to be perfect to be an economic evangelist. Perfection is striving for excellence. God is not looking for perfect people to do a perfect work. He uses Imperfect people to do a perfect work. Kings and Queens are the Joshua and David of today using their gifts and talents as a resource to get people to the source, God (Jesus). As I stated earlier in the book, Kings and Queens go into the hedges and highways, workplace to share the true gospel. That Jesus is the truth the way and the life. Our job is not to judge, but to give life.

Matthew 13: 33 says, "**The kingdom of heaven is like yeast that a woman took and mixed into a large amount of floor until it worked all through the dough**". Yeast is used here as a symbol of growth. When you start your own business or ministry the key is to grow. Although the kingdom began small and was nearly invisible, it will soon grow and have great impact on the world. The book of Matthew has many parables on the kingdom, but Matthew 13:47-49, best describes who economic evangelists are. It says, "**Once again the kingdom of heaven is like a <u>Net that was let down into the lake (Marketplace)</u> and caught all kinds of fish. When it was full, the fishermen pulled it up on the shore. Then they sat down and collected the good fish in baskets, but threw the bad away. This is how it will be at the end of the age. The angels will come and separate the wicked from the righteous**". This parable is about fishing net, The Holy Spirit reveled to me, that the net represents "**Networking**".

7

Networking: Economic Empowerment

When you mention the word networking, lots of people know the word, but don't know the language. Networking is bigger than what you think. Sally networks with Jim, Jim networks with Gary etc…Networking can work many different ways. Networks are the richest companies in the world. Look at CBS, ESPN, NBC, ABC, these are powerhouse money-making networks.

Let's start with network marketing (also known as multilevel marketing or MLM) Just saying the words conjures up a lot of emotions for most people. You either love it or you hate it. Sometimes both. But just what is it? Have you ever been to a great movie or a great restaurant or a sale is going on in the mall, you tell a friend that's networking. The church that you attend how did you get there? Networking is basically word of mouth marketing. Most people talk about networking as a bad thing, but what they don't realize it's the best money making in the world. We do networking all the time for almost every product or service we use—and we do it for free! In network marketing, which I now call economic evangelism, you are paid for doing this form of advertising on a **residual income** basis.

8

What is Residual Income?

Residual income, is income you continue to earn for a long period of time as a result of marketing a product or service **once**? Example: when you first activated your power for your house you only did it once and you have to pay that bill every month or your power will get turned off. The same is true with a networking opportunity, you continue to make money from that product or service every time you or someone in your organization, whom you may or may not know sells (markets) it to a customer—that you also don't know. You can receive money for work you did weeks months, or years earlier, when you evangelize to someone else to become part of your **network**. The person evangelized someone else to become part of their network (and therefore part of your network), and the new person sold the product or service to the customer—who may also become part of that person's network, and part of your network. The person may become a customer—they buy and use the product or service or they may become a business builder and go out to add more people to their network and yours. You continue to be rewarded for the work you did in the past to bring others into the business. That's how God works!

The name of my company is Maycomm Marketing. Maycomm Marketing is a company that offers benefits to businesses, families and individuals. One service we offer is healthcare benefits for people who cannot afford, cannot qualify or has pre-existing conditions. The benefits gives you the same access to healthcare without paying the middleman (Insurance company) a high monthly premium, but you get the same care for $109 a month. Every membership we sale, we profit up front $112 per sale per week. For example if we sold 5 this week we made $560, not bad for maybe 20 hours of work. But my point is that the next month even if we don't sale anything, we still get paid a residual income of $12.00 times those 5 sales, which equals $60.00 every month. I know that's not much money, but just imagine 100 sales or more times $12.00? We still get paid every month from a one-time effort, not including new sales that month!

In other kinds of commissioned selling, such as the work of real estate agents or car sales people, the person doing the marketing and making the sale gets paid only once. There are no residual incomes from selling a house or car. Are you getting paid from your job what you did last year?

In networking, an average everyday person like you and I can create a residual income stream by word of mouth advertising of a company's product or services. Residual income recipients like insurance agents require unique or special talent or education or both to earn their money. Don't get me wrong, I have a four-year degree in communications, from Lees McRae College. As I stated earlier God was a smart worker. In net-working you don't need a degree or any special talent but the ability to speak (talk) and help other people earn residual income. The more leaders you help develop, the more money you are going to make. Residual income is the only way I've ever seen which ensures that you will have the money to enjoy your free time. Most people you and I know enjoy either free time or plenty of money or neither, but not both.

I believe and know God created residual income for the men and women of God to yes have more free time and enjoy the abundant life but more to do ministry for His kingdom.

9

That's a Pyramid Thing?

Every time I approach someone, and introduce a business opportunity, the first thing they say is that's one of those "pyramids". This is the most frequently asked question in networking. What they are really trying to say is, isn't pyramids illegal? NO, networking isn't illegal. Nor are all pyramids—structured business illegal. Let me explain. Every company, the U.S. government, and virtually any organization of any kind use a pyramid organizational structure. In a company there is usually one president, several senior vice presidents, then vice presidents of different departments or areas of the world. Senior managers, managers, and assistant managers. How many layers exist in this pyramid structure depends in part on how big the company is, but employees are always at the bottom of the company pyramid.

The same goes for the church, where God is the head, directly to him is a Bishop, or Pastor, and the heads of each ministry report directly to him or members of his pastoral care. You can see that the pyramid structure not only works, but it's also normally perfectly **legal** and is accepted without a second thought.

A pyramid-structured business can be **illegal** under certain conditions. When the structure is used for the purposes that are illegal under the law. That's what's meant when someone talks about illegal pyramid schemes and they are indeed schemes, created with the intent that those on top will make all the money and others who participate never figure it out. That's the kind of organization that has given the term "pyramid" a bad name.

Federal law defines an **illegal** pyramid as a business venture where a person must make an investment to get the right to recruit others into a company. Such a person receives money solely from recruiting people. The new recruits must make an investment. There is no ongoing or residual income the new recruits make money from others when they recruit others to join.

All these conditions must be in place for the law to consider a business an illegal pyramid.

A simple definition of an illegal pyramid is a business where money is made from signing up **new people** rather than by marketing and selling **legitimate products** or services to end-user consumers.

An example of an illegal pyramid is when someone asks you to invest $1000. In exchange the person tells you that if you recruit two people to each invest $1000, and each of those two people gets two people to invest $1000, and of those four people now gets two people each to invest $1000, you will then be paid $14,000, when you reach the top of the money tree. Why? Fourteen people are in your money down-line each paying $1000 for their spot in the pyramid, in hope that they will also get to the top of the money pyramid.

This is illegal pyramid because:

1. Those at the bottom of the pyramid will get burned.

2. No legitimate product or service is being sold.

3. You are being paid only for recruiting others.

THAT'S Illegal!

10

Linear Income verses Residual Income.

I have been in business for eight years. I have also during those years worked part-time jobs to supplement my business for tax purposes, which I will share with you in another chapter. What is linear income? Most people you know and maybe yourself works 9 to 5 or some hourly shift. This is called linear income, working time for the exchange for money. I am here to tell you that working time for money all your life will never give you time freedom or wealth. The secret of the wealthy is not that they have more money, but that they have more freedom because many of their streams are residual income. But many groups of people are not as wealthy as they appear. Doctors and dentists don't earn residual income from their labors. Their income potential is capped. They can see only a fixed number of patients in a day, and they have to be there for every single one. The same holds true for the top salespeople, chiropractors, and attorneys. Most of them don't enjoy the power of residual income either. They appear to be rich, but they're on a treadmill just like most people. Don't be deceitful of wealth, as it talks about in **Mark 4:18-19, "Now these are the ones sown among thorns; they are the ones who hear the word, and the cares of this world, deceitfulness of riches, and the *desires for other things choke the word, and it becomes unfruitful"*.**

The bible also says, **"In all things get understanding"**. After you read this book please share this **information** to everybody you come in contact with. What percentage of your income is residual? If you're smart after reading this book, you'll start shifting your income streams from linear to residual. This will give you the time freedom to do more for the kingdom and yourself. This can happen with starting on at least one new residual stream every year!

www.maycomm.cjb.net

11

The power of Duplication

The bible opens with God (Gen. 1:1). The first thing we read about God is that He created the heavens and the earth. In other words, God first appears in scripture as a *worker.* As I stated earlier in the book, consider the many kinds of work that God did in forming the world: artist, designer, strategic planner, organizer, project developer, zoologist, biologist. Chemist, to name but a few. He created us in his own image, so it's our job to be Christ like. We may never take on the many works as He, but we **must finish** what He started. There are three types of work: **work, work hard and work smart.** God worked smart. Everything He made He spoke it in six days, and on the seventh day He rested. Rest simply means, ceases from working. He put everything on autopilot. God also created Adam and Eve to become co-workers along with you and me to oversee the earth. We are His co-workers, called to accomplish meaningful task. How can we accomplish this task? After God created male and female, He blessed them and said **"Be fruitful and multiply"**, not meaning just having babies, but go **duplicate** His work and build up more kingdom builders. (Economic Evangelist)

The same concept God wants us to do in building up the kingdom applies to your ministry, business and place of work. Duplication will happen, when you take your God given abilities, knowledge, work styles and motivation to help others. Building a network of people, who are working in a similar manner, creates a more productive and efficient organization than would be possible if that person and everyone else were working on his or her own. Duplicating yourself is an ongoing process. It continues for many months, perhaps years. You're always looking for more economic evangelist to duplicate yourself, just make sure what your duplicating is of God. "For only what you do for God will last".

12

Tax "Tips" and Advantages of Owning a Business

Would you believe that our government knows a great secret and they won't tell you! No! If you would like to increase your available of "take-home" pay and greatly reduce your taxes forever; you have to start a "home-based" business! Can you believe that the government will actually pay you to have your own "e-biz" that's "incredible"! (**www.may-comm.cjb.net**)

The Benefits are outstanding

In fact, you can deduct your spouse, your children, and a part of your house and your auto, your vacation (anywhere in the world) and approximately 138 more tax deductions. The car I drive today, the government paid for it. How? I deducted it from my income. You can even set up a pension plan that blows social security and any other government plan away! The main thing to do is take action and do it right!

You will never lose a business deduction!

If you are an employee and you also own a "home-based" business that isn't making money yet, you can use these "**paper losses**" to offset against any other income that you have including your actual employee earnings, dividends pensions interest and even your spouse's taxable income provided you're filing jointly!

<u>The key is to make it a business, NOT a hobby!</u>

You must treat your business as a business if you want to deduct all of your expenses. So get serious and you will really love the incredible tax advantages and benefits you will be getting!

Here are a few important points to keep in mind!

$ Successful business people keep good tax records and business diaries.

$ Successful business people keep an adequate inventory (If applicable).
If you are involved in an internet-based "e-biz', your company may or may not require you to stock some product to show. Most "e-companies" offer services such as tax audit protection, websites, "on-line" computer training, internet tool boxes which provide you with tools you will need to make money on the web, **www.maycomm.cjb.net**, etc…

$ Successful business people are excited about their product and/or services because they use them. They know they will have a stronger belief in their products and/or services if they have their own testimonials.

$ Successful business people attend training seminars and/or business briefings and listen to audiotapes about their business. They also watch training videos to keep themselves well educated on their "e-company's" product and/or services

$ Successful business people work their business a minimum of 8 hours per week consistently. I personally believe you need to work 40 hours per week if you're just starting, for "survival" unless you are using the business while working your job as an asset.

$ I have been in business for eight years and have never given up! Successful business people never give up. Winners never quit, and quitters never win! They keep trying to make money. You can deduct weddings and education how would you like to deduct the cost of your children's weddings and education? Sounds great, doesn't it? You can do it. If you do it right! If you hire your children to help you in your business, their wages will be tax-deductible.

Example: Gary, Mike, Tilara and Curtis are teenage children of Jerry and Clara. If Jerry and Clara have to save $5,000 per year for their college education, none of the $20,000 per year is tax deductible! That's not good! However, if jerry and Clara hire their four children to perform business services for them such as addressing, passing out flyers or taking calls etc…they can receive the equivalent of a tax deduction for the $20,000 in employee wages. In essence, this is the same exact money jerry and Clara was saving for their four children's college education but now it all becomes tax-deductible as wages. Another great benefit is that if you hire your children who are under the age of 18 in your self-employed business, the children's income are exempt from federal unemployment tax and social security tax. Also, the first $3,900 per year that you pay each child is tax-free from income taxes! Remember also consult with your tax professional!

In summary, starting your own business is your ticket to wealth, not just 9 to 5! After you finish reading this book, email or call me to help start your business or ministry to grow financially.

13

Business owner—verses—Business Investor

The three types of work are once again, work, work hard and work smart. **Work** just simply means you have a job, you may not like it but it pays the bills or you take what you can get. **Work hard,** just means maybe you have a good job or business, but work 90 hours a week, but never have any free time! **Work smart** means working less time, but making more money or money working for you, not you working for **all** the money! Your money now becomes an employee working hard to make more money! That's a **business investor**, they let money work for them, while a **business owner** works most of the time for his money. Business Investors build and acquire assets even if they work in fast food? Real assets fall into several different categories:

1. Businesses that do not require my presence. I own them, but they are managed or run by other people (Networking). If I have to work there, it's not a business. It becomes my job.

2. Stocks

3. Bonds

4. Mutual funds

5. Income—generating real estate

6. Royalties like this book, music

7. Anything else that value produces income or appreciates.

I use to be a business owner, but God has given me the wisdom to go from a business owner to becoming a business investor. From 1996 to 1999 I owned two wireless communication stores. With owning the stores I had to either be in the stores to make money or hire someone to run them while I was gone. This is called overhead. Instead of the business running without my presence, I had to pay someone or close the store and make no money! Well the experience I learned in running a business, as a business owner taught me how to become business minded, but a business minded investor. Today I invest in many low small business opportunities that pay high returns, letting my money work for me. For example, back in 1998 I invested $99.00 in a healthcare savings company, and for the past two years I have not worked the business at all, and I have received a check every month for about $200, that's $2400 a year with zero hours! That's what I mean, when I say money working for you as a business investor.

14

Make it, but also save it!

The key to financial planning is cash—flow management. You've not only got to get the cash to flow into your reservoir, but you have to manage the leaks so that there is money left over at the end of the month. This monthly surplus is the secret to financial growth. The surplus can be invested. The object of the money game is to accumulate enough investments so that the income from these investments will eventually support you. Next you need to save your surplus. There are two meanings for the word **save:** (1) to pay less for your purchases, (2) to create a surplus, as in "I need to save some money for retirement." Some people are good at the first save. They like to shop for bargains. But they are terrible at the second save. Wealthy people are great at both.

Another benefit my company offers is a debt management program. We show you how to turn your everyday debt, into wealth. (**www.maycommmoneycenter.cjb.net**) For example: anyone can save money by buying at a discount, but do they save the money that they save? That's the hard part. Everybody will not be a millionaire, but everybody can become wealthy. For an example: A customer of mine was paying $400 a month in health insurance, and only went to the doctor maybe twice a year. I helped them save about $300 a month because the health-care savings program we offer is only $109.00 a month. There are two things my customer can do. First, save the $300 a month and invest it to make more money to pay off other debt! OR second spend it. The bible says, **"If you will be faithful over a few things, God will make you ruler over many".** What could you do with an extra $3600 a year? Check your debt and see if you can turn it into wealth. By just changing buying habits will change your financial situation. **"Money saved is as good as money**

gained." But one more thing, pay **yourself first,** but only if your bills are paid. God gets 10% off top, then pay yourself 10%. Every month, you pay your creditors, the Phone Company, the electric company and everyone else. But what's in it for you? The key to successful investing is to pay you. Every week I have 10% of my check automatically withdrawn from my personal account into my brokerage account. Make it automatic, like you owe yourself the money and you won't even miss it. Just like your weekly paycheck, your employer deducts 7.5% straight off the top of your pay-check for FICA, SOCIAL SECURITY AND MEDICARE. You don't miss it because you can't touch it. Imagine you took that same 7.5% con-tribution straight off top of your paycheck and invested it each month into retirement or investment account and into the Kingdom?

15

Financial Independence

What is financial independence? This book with the aid of the Holy Spirit is to help you open your mind to create financial independence. By financial independence I mean freedom from worry about money. Financial independence will enable you to do more ministry and enjoy the abundant life. Your progress towards financial independence is very easy to measure and calculate how many days; months or years you will be able to maintain your current standard of living based on the amount of money you choose to bring in. If you quit your job or business completely, how long could you survive on what you saved on right now? If you were to cut back to working just a few days a week, would you pay the bills and enjoy yourself?

Financial independence does not necessarily equal "retirement". Retirement means working with no intention of going back. While retirement may come with financial independence, that's a choice only you can make. Financial independence to me is the ability to wake up in the morning and decide what you want to do, without being forced to do something you don't want to do for money.

16

Security Verses Freedom

Ask yourself do I really have freedom? This is America, land of the free and home of the brave. You remember that song? Well let me tell you, that song is very old. Most people maybe even you think security and freedom are the same word. They are not. In fact, in many ways, security and freedom mean exactly the opposite things. For example parents and teachers want their kids to get good grades for job security, hopefully a high paying job. But school is not really about freedom; it's about job security. By now you should have figured out that there is no such thing as job security. As a matter of fact you can't have both working just 9 to 5! If you still have the mindset of living off of social security or money you might have put into a 401k plan. Get ready for a rude awakening in the future. Right now your mind set should becoming business minded, building up assets. People who depend upon social security are some of the poorest people in America and with least freedom. Just in case you still don't get the picture, let me paint one for you. The more you have of one (security or freedom), the less you have of the other. In fact the more security you have, the more trapped you become. Here is the picture. Just look at the people in the world who have the most security. They're called prison inmates. They have a house, food, free time, exercise yard, but they have no freedom. Is this the path your own? You either have faith or fear. Faith equals freedom, fear equals security. Which one do you want? **Once upon a time**, all a person had to do was go to school, get good grades, find a safe secure job, be a loyal employee, retire, move to a smaller house on a golf course, and live happily ever after. But just like that old song I mention in the beginning of this chapter, that is today an old fairy tale. We as economic evangelist must be prepared, and prepare all of Gods people for the storm that's coming.

17

The storm (ERISA)

What is ERISA? It stands for **Employee Retirement Income Security Act.** It was the act that made 401ks possible in 1974. This act was passed to help protect employees' retirement money from abuse by their business owners. What kind of abuse? Do you remember the Enron and MCI scandals? That kind of abuse is why ERISA was put into place. The act was passed as a benefit for employees, a way to protect employees, but we all know, nothing is only good for only one group of people. The company also benefited from the act, but the benefits to the company were not really mentioned in the press. Because of hidden taxes the employees are often not even aware of most companies can not pay more to there retirement plan. Every time an employee gets a raise the government also gets a raise. So while ERISA was passed as a benefit to employees, it was in many ways more of a benefit to the employer. Meaning the expense of retirement has transferred from the employer to the employee.

Storm ERISA is a financial storm. It will be like hurricane HUGO or FLOYD when it actually hits home in the near future. ERISA will be caused by millions of people who have invested money in 401ks. How? Because millions of people have put money into the market are not investors. Most can't read a financial statement. So how can you invest if you cannot read a financial statement? So they will be depending on their financial future to the stock market, and we all know that all markets go up and all markets go down. The problem will be that most employees do not have mental and emotional training and if another tragedy happens like 911, they will act like most untrained investors. Panic and begin selling, selling to save their lives, selling to protect their future. I am not tell-

33

ing you not to invest in a 401k plan. But what I am saying is, become an educated investor, don't just depend on a stockbroker to take care of your retirement, become financially literate for yourself. ERSIA will being to hit home around 2010 if it's the Lord will to let me and you see it. I am 31 years old and most of my generation will not have enough money to retire on. Why? 75 million baby boomers will be retiring and instead of putting money in a 401k plan 75 million will be pulling out, that may cause the biggest stock market crash ever. My question to you is will you be ready, or will you be like the people back in Noah's day? If this ERSIA storm hits home you will notice that the people being left behind financially are often the people stuck in old ways of thinking and doing things. That is why you must start now building a financial ark.

18

Building a Financial Ark!

If you want to be a wealthy business owner or investor, you need to understand the story of Noah and the Ark. Do you realize how much faith it took for Noah to go to his family and say, "God told me there is a great flood coming, so we need to build an ark. I started writing this book in the year of 2001. After I did a seminar in front of about 500 people. God dropped in my spirit to tell his people just like Noah; it's going to rain. No not a physical rain, but financially. But only for those who hears the call, and starts to build their financial ark will survive. He told me to tell everybody that I came in contact with, through seminars and one on one. But still today, 2003, people still don't seem to get the picture, even after seeing Enron, MCI, and many others fall.

I am going to preach and teach financial salvation until people all across this nation wakes up to what God is doing for the sake of the "righteous". The fall of all these fortune 500 companies was not the work of the devil, but of God. God is trying to get his people as the head and not the tail in these last days. God is trying to open up more of your mind because that's were money is made? With my mind? Yes! With all the chaos you think you have been through financially it's just a set up. For your mind to come up with creative godly ideas to make money. Think about it, ideas are formed in your mind first, then put into place to make money. The point I am trying to make is the ark you need to be making financially is in your head. If money is not found in your head it will not be found in your hands. As an economic evangelist you must be prepared to prepare. Noah could not get all the animals on board, and the same is true with most people you will minister to, but you must still preach and teach the message.

35

Building a financial ark in your head will save you and make you a wealthy person in a good or bad economy.

19

The Internet: Your Money making machine!

The Internet. How many times have you heard that word this week? One of the greatest money making in the world. It's not a fad. I could quote you numbers about how many hundreds of millions of people are online or coming online, but this thing is moving so fast that by the time you read this page any numbers will be crazy. The Internet is a tidal wave. You can ride this wave to fortune or be left way behind. Are you on the Net yet? If not, stop reading right now and get hooked up. It's that important. Go. I don't want you to be left behind. If you're already hooked up, fire up your computer right now. We're going for a drive on the **"information"** superhighway. All the business opportunities I invest in have a website. Websites to me are like real estate, the more I have, and the more cash flow I have. Get the picture? As I stated in Chapter 1, people, businesses, and Churches are not growing because of tradition. Let's compare traditional marketing tools with Internet marketing.

Traditional Marketing	*Internet Marketing*
Postal Mail—slow, expensive	E-mail (fast, cheap)
High mailing cost	Zero mailing cost
Long delivery time	instantaneous delivery time
Business week/hours	24/7/365
Limited customers	Unlimited customers
High overhead	Almost Zero

Traditional Marketing	Internet Marketing
High entry costs	Low entry costs
Dress up/office	Stay home in your T-shirt
Local area	Entire world
Fixed Location	Seen from any computer
Uncool	Cool

As you can see marketing is the oxygen of any business. Without it, you won't be in business very long. In the regular world, marketing is expensive, one of your largest business expenses. When I was a retail business owner, marketing and overhead took half of my profit. The experiences I have had in the traditional way of running a business was very time consuming with a very low profit margin. Even though I grossed over $400,000, a lot of it went out the door. You do know that it's not what you earn it's what you keep. With Internet marketing you will invest low and get a high return. Internet marketing makes it possible for you to reach new customers for pennies per thousand versus hundreds of dollars per thousand. When you get a chance check out my healthcare website (www.**maycommbenefits**.cjb.net), see how easy it is to view to help customers purchase a membership right in the comfort of their home without my presence. For example I run small classified ads with my web address and receive checks in the mail weekly without even talking to the customer. Can you see how the Internet is a cash-making machine?

I wrote this book wanting to help future economic evangelist share the good news. But also to help the under paid people earn an additional $500 or $1000 a month working part-time. Because, even $500 extra will change the lives of maybe 95% of the people in the entire world!

I am also hoping that while you read this book, that "Lazarus" business idea will raise up inside of you. The Internet is the way for your idea to be seen every where at any given time. What I hope to do in this book is to show non-dreamers how easy it is to make a few thousand here and there playing with Network Marketing. Hoping that when they tasted this extra money on top of their job or business they'd go for more. But at the same time helping others lost in the rat race do the same. This is what economic evangelism is all about. But even tough you show non-dreamers real paychecks you have made outside of a 9 to 5 job most will still stay in the bondage. Don't be offended by them, understand them and pray for them. Most are conservatives, or naïve wage—earners, who have no earthly conception of how Networking works, could Never, in their wildest dream reason that anyone other than movie stars, CEO's of giant corporations, star athletes, or dope dealers could make six figures or extra income without two and three jobs. These folks you can never convince. They really would not believe you, if you told them you could make **stock option** trades without a stock broker on the internet, making 10% to 40% **monthly** returns with a click of a button! (www.tradewithandy.com)

20

Rental Stock or Covered Call Stock Option: Money making Money!

In this chapter pay close attention, you're about to go to another level financially. What's a stock option? Well there are two types of stock options. First is a **Call Option**, which is the right, but not the obligation, to buy a certain number of shares of a certain stock, at a certain price (strike price) for a specific time period (time periods expire on the third Friday of the month). Second is a **Put Option**, which is the right, but not the obligation, to sell a certain number of shares of a certain stock, at a certain price (strike price) for a specific time period. A lot of people will tell you, that's not educated on stock options, that they are risky. But options were formed to reduce the risk. The risk is limited to the cost of the option. For example: A person purchases 1000 shares of a ($20) stock for $20,000. If the stock price falls to ($10) the stock value would be $10,000 less. A person buys ten (10) **call option** contracts (1000 shares)

For one dollar ($1) each equals $1,000, if the stock price falls to ($10) he or she only loses the $1000 paid for the **Option** by letting it expire. You got it so far? The stockowner suffers a loss if the stock price falls, and the **Option Owner** allows the option to expire, losing only the $1000 price paid for the option. Now would you rather lose $10,000 or $1000 if you would lose? But look at the positive side, if the stock price goes up, the Option Owner earns the same as if he or she owned the stock. Example: Once again you purchased 1000 shares of $20 stock for $20,000. If the stock price went up to $25, you would make $5000 (25% on your investment). But the best thing that you need to know is Options create leverage. Example: If you purchased an **option** to buy 10 call contracts at $20 **strike price** (1000 shares) for one dollar each ($1) for $1000. If the stock price went up to $25, you would make the same $5000 profit (500% on your investment). The point I am really trying to show you is there are stock option **sellers and buyers**. You want to be on the side of selling, which is called **covered calls.**

Covered calls simply means you own the stock, so you can sell an **Option** to someone else and earn some immediate short-term income every month.

Why should I consider such a plan? Well, the obvious benefit, is that instead of working hard hoping that your 401k are going to give you a great return on your money in the long run. Why not sell options and make more money? I have a 401k at my job, but I also have my own online brokerage account that I invest most of money to work hard to make more money. As you have read in earlier chapters, you must become financially literate and stop depending on a broker or 401k through your job, learn and earn for yourself. Check out this quote from a financial planner to a client: "I've reviewed your financial picture, and if **we** manage your money properly, there should be plenty for **both of us**". This is why you have to become financially literate about your own financial future.

The best thing about stock options is you can make 3% to 40% or more returns on your money monthly. Will your bank do that? As a matter of fact your bank does the same trading methods with your money and gives you 3% a year. How? To show you how this works, lets pretend that you have invested $5 in 1,000 shares of XYZ Company. That means your portfolio is worth $5,000. Since you own the stock you can sell an option every month to someone else. There are people willing to give you 50 cents a share today for the right to buy a call option at $6 a share. That could generate $500 in income immediately in your own brokerage account (1,000 shares x $0.50 = $500). This is an 8.3 percent on your money ($500/$5,000 = 8.3%), as you can see how powerful this is, you don't have to wait an entire year as you do with your bank. These are the kinds of returns the banks are getting monthly with your money. For more information on stock options visit **www.optionxpress.com** also sign up here to get your free online brokerage account with checkbook.

21

Pastors and Marketplace leaders Partnership

✦

(1 Samuel 9:1, 15:31)

1 Samuel 9: 1–15:31, paints a marvelous picture of how pastors and economic leaders can partner together to fulfill a God—given vision. First Samuel shows how God sovereignty uses both Samuel the priest (Ministry leader) and Saul the king (Marketplace leader). Because he feels secure, Samuel is able to fulfill his role as a spiritual leader to big and strong Saul. He finds his security in his divine call and in the one who called him, not in people. While Saul could be an intimidating, daunting role, nor can he be diverted from his work in Saul's life. Observe the partnership of these two in fulfilling God's plan.

1. Samuel could speak into Saul's life because he felt secure in his calling (9: 17-19). While God told Samuel to anoint Saul as King, the prophet never considered the son of Kish to be a celebrity. Saul because King over Samuel—but never placed his security or emotional health in a mere man. With poise and confidence he said to Saul, "I am the prophet". He then instructed Saul concerning the spiritual matters he would face as king.

2. Samuel affirmed Saul's complementary role and honored him for it (9:21-23). Although Samuel had been the visible leader in Israel, he intentionally gave away his status by publicly honoring Saul. He

reserved special food for him and a special place at the table, so no one would question who they were to follow.

3. Samuel anointed Saul for the role he was to fulfill (10:1). Samuel didn't feel competition or envy over this new king; He knew that both would serve as leaders among God's people as complementary partners. We are not to compete with each other, but to complete each other.

4. Samuel helped Saul to receive a new heart for serving people (10:6-9). At this point Samuel had every reason to feel awkward or displaced; now Saul was doing the very thing Samuel had been gifted to do. But Samuel didn't resist helping Saul to develop into the spiritual leader God called him to be.

5. Samuel encouraged Saul to use his spiritual gifts (10:10-13) Samuel faithfully brought God's word to Saul. He prepared Saul to receive his spiritual gifts by explaining what would happen and when to look for it.

6. Samuel did not feel intimidated by or envious of Saul's conquest (13:8-13) Samuel allowed neither Saul's position as King nor his success as conqueror to move him. While Samuel affirmed the King, he also understood his role in Israel and in the King's life. Samuel confronted Saul's disobedience and clarified each of their roles.

7. Samuel spoke words of direction to Saul (15:1-3) even after confronting Saul's disobedience, Samuel was able to provide direction for the King and affirm his work on the battlefield. He didn't shrink from playing his role in Saul's life and again clarified Saul's place in the scheme of things. He furnished Saul with great confidence and support as he led the armies of Israel.

8. Samuel prayed and hurt for Saul when the King failed (15:10,11). Samuel grieved when God rejected the disobedient Saul. He knew

that God intended great things for Saul—and the King's failure broke Samuel's heart. As Saul's spiritual leader, Samuel hurt for the King.

9. Samuel could confront Saul when he sinned and provide him perspective (15:12-23) Samuel felt called to continually provide the big picture perspective to Saul and remind him of his roots of God's call and mission. He offered an eternal perspective to the King and refused to let him try to do God's will in his own way.

10. Samuel possessed the spiritual credibility to call for repentance and worship from Saul (15:24-31). Samuel ministered to Saul with a beautiful combination of grace and truth. He spoke the truth in love, never out of spite or superiority. And when he returned with Saul, he did it not out of intimidation, but to leave Saul with as much dignity as possible.

As an economic evangelist, it is very important to form a partnership with your Pastor. I know and believe that when marketplace leaders and pastor can work together as a team, then you'll see a change in your local ministry financially. I am talking about getting your people Pastors in your Church blessed before you think about building a dome! After all we are the Church and if the Church is broke and the Pastor is Fat paid not from business deals outside the Church? How do you expect the ministry to grow? I know some Pastor probably want like what I am saying but the truth is the truth. Don't just ask for money, money, and money, give your people a vision, and never equip and teach them in economic development so they can make more money. All I am trying to say is the more economically developed a local Church body you have will determine the power you have financially. I believe every ministry should be empowering their people economically. A Church that is financially empowered does not need a benevolent fund, because the people in the Church become a benevolent fund. If you're reading this book and you know this book will bless your ministry, call or email me for an economic development workshop. (**kbcceo@aol.com**)

22

The World's New Global Marketplace: Foreign Currency!

Your way of making money and investing should change with time. Now is the time to discover the Foreign Exchange Market. Think about it? Where are most of America's jobs moving? Yes you got it over seas. So if that is where the jobs are going why are you not going there. No I am not talking about physically, but your money. How?

This is the twenty-first century, the world has indeed gotten smaller. This decrease has been magnified by the global use of computers. What use to require a week to send to Europe or Asia now only requires a few seconds. And, needless to say, computers have changed the way companies do business. The list of changes goes on and on; however, our main concern is the new freedom given to you, King and Queens to invest in the foreign market. This market, in the past (60,70, 80's) had been the sole domain of major banks; other large financial institutions and central banks, such as the U.S. Federal Reserve Bank. The substantial profits made annually by these institutions from trading in the foreign market is now offered to you, in large part due to recent changes in international laws.

Economic Background

Just like Chapter 20, Pastors and Economic Evangelist need partnership, the same is true with countries. The increase in global and foreign investments has made the economics of all countries more dependent upon one another. A country's currency fluctuates as a result of economic activity. Historical events such as the fall of communism in the soviet Union and

Eastern Europe, the continuing liberalization of Chinese economy, the political reform in South America have, and the development of common currency in Europe opened up a new market for individual investors.

How does one explain the price moves in the foreign currency? There are several major factors, and many less important ones, but they have something ridiculously obvious in common: The foreign exchange markets move when some force makes one currency either more or less valuable the another.

Economic factors usually affect a currency by altering the interests rate structure of the country. Many economists would be more general, saying that a currency depends on the goods, services, and assets denominated in that currency. The interest rate structure of a country could reflect perhaps an even more important structure—the overall monetary health of that country.

The FOREX Market Today

As an Economic Evangelist, you must catch hold not only how to make money, but be a pioneer to the shift of how money works in the world. Foreign exchange is the backbone of all international capital transactions. The majority of deals are speculative. Even if we add tens of billions of dollars of daily bond switching, foreign exchange business is still 10 times greater than is required for trade and investments purposes. In other words, for every trade or investment related deal, there are nine speculative ones. Compared to the wafer-thin profit margins in other areas of commercial banking, the largest profits from minor exchange movements in a matter of minutes seem to good to pass by.

Trading volume has been growing at a rate of least 25% per year since the 1980's. It is therefore not difficult to accept the proposition that foreign exchange is the world's fastest growing industry. Some banks make 40%–60% of their profits trading currencies with your money. In the August 1994 issue of the International Finance Magazine, Charles Sanford, Chairman of Bankers Trust, expressed his opinion that by the year 2020; banks will cease their loan transaction business, and focus on currency trading as their primary revenue source. So why are you King and Queen largely unknown to the FOREX market? The answer is simple, until recently, over-the counter currency market was simply financially inaccessible for the general population of investors and traders, and the minimum account requirements were beyond the resources of average individual investor. Since we live in what Dr. Wanda A. Turner calls the "Up side down Kingdom", meaning the first shall be last, and the last shall be first. Suddenly instead of minimum investment of $200k, accounts can be opened from lows as $300 to $50k. This market does not have a single physical location such as trading exchange. Rather, it is a global network of banks, investment banks and brokerage houses that comprise an electronically linked infrastructure servicing international corporations, banks and investment funds by trading currencies, offsetting the risk of currency rate fluctuations and taking speculative trading positions to realize the profit from the second-by second fluctuating currency exchange rates. Millions of dollars are moved from one currency into another every second of the day, by virtue of a simple phone conversation.

Instead of attempting to choose a particular stock out of thousands available in the equity markets, the foreign currency exchange deals primarily with 4 to 10 different currencies. The approach to understanding this market is substantially different, in that its involvement in the global competition of the nations, and it's obscure international games of big money, where the participants rarely care about a 200 point drop in the Dow Jones, simply because its impact will have no bearing on the global over the counter currency market.

It is only an informed few inspired by the Holy Sprit that effectively invest and continue to earn even while they play or rest. Listen to me good I am not telling you to get excited about trading stock options and the FOREX market without more education and money. Stock options and the FOREX market can bring wealth to you quickly. But the high returns also have a large degree of risk. Only discretionary income should be used (OVERFLOW) for such investment purposes. Make sure before you make any investment that you consult **God** to what He would want you to do with His money. Also let me kill a demon while you read this book. I can here some of the religious, Bible carrying, tongue talking saints saying this is gambling. Let me bust your bubble and tell you to read your Bible, because trading is in the Bible, read Matthew 25, the parable of the talents.

As an economic evangelist arm yourself with the facts about the present opportunities in world-wide markets. Take charge of your future today and be prepared to act. Study as the word of God says and it will determine your level of financial freedom tomorrow. After all, we are all right where we have insisted upon being. As I stated early in the book we are in the Information age, and for more Information visit www.4xmadeeasy.com.

23

Take action now!

Economic evangelist are people of action. Who are financially literate reaching out to minister financial salvation out side of the four walls of the Church, but it must start from the inside of the Church out into the marketplace. Economic evangelist are people ministering with people, who minister with people, who minister with people, who minister with more people, etc…It's a whole line of people ministering people to salvation as well as financial salvation.

All of us were given two great gifts: our mind and our time. It is up to you to do what you please with both. With each dollar that enters your hand, you and only you have the power to determine your destiny. If you choose to keep doing what you been doing, then let me tell you, your going to keep getting what you have been getting. Spend your money and time foolishly, you choose to be poor. Spend it on liabilities, you join the middle class. Invest in yourself, in your mind and learn how to acquire assets and you will be choosing wealth as your goal and your future. Choose to share this knowledge with your friends, family, and Church, you choose to prepare them for the world that waits. No one else will. But as I said in the introduction of this book, it's a book about money, but not all about money. But living the life of an economic evangelist, is a life of Faith. There is another choice that's more important than any dollar or investment you could ever make. That choice is **HEAVEN** or **HELL**, which one have you chose? You can make all the money in the world, but until you invite **JESUS CHRIST** into your life that money will never bring you fulfillment. Jesus is the best investment I have ever made. Without Jesus you can't be an economic evangelist, you might have the form, but not the power. I will end this book saying without **salvation**, you can't have **financial salvation**. Stop praying to God for money; pray to God for His favor. I wish you great wealth much happiness and Gods speed.

Gary Mayes (Romans 10:9)

Testimony

Subj: Information on credit report!
Date: 10/8/2003 5:41 PM Eastern Daylight Time
From: Lcrenshaw@ yahoo.com
To: Kbcceo@aol.com
Sent from the Internet (Details)

Hello my name is Lee Crenshaw; I'm 23 years old. Thanks to Gary's credit advise, wisdom counseling and especially his credit solutions web site www.maycommmoneycenter.cjb.net, I am on my way to a great CREDIT SCORE and even better, a brighter financial future. Like us all when we were in our teens, we all did at least one or two stupid things that we regretted. Yes I was stupid my mistake was that I royally messed up my credit report up beyond repair. There was no hope for seven long years. I maxed my first credit card out, never paid a single bill on it and of course it went on my credit report. I couldn't even get a checking account. I lost all hope until I met Gary Mayes. I met Gary in May of 2003 at our place of employment. He told me a way that I could clear bad items off my credit report. This guy is for real. Take it from me! Gary explained me something called the FCRA (Fair Credit Reporting Act) His site gave me the necessary tools to dispute negative information off my credit report. Within the first 30 days I had my 2000 repossession deleted off my Equifax credit report, within the first 60 days I have had 11 more negative items deleted off my credit report. Gary is not just a good teacher when it comes to your credit; he is also a great person. Gary knows what he is talking about and his tools and tips really work.

0-595-31605-0